WHAT
YOU
SHOULD
KNOW
ABOUT
MARY

WHAT
YOU
SHOULD
KNOW
ABOUT

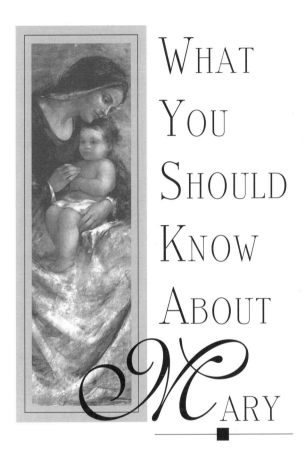

$\mathcal{M}$ARY

CHARLENE ALTEMOSE, MSC

Liguori

ONE LIGUORI DRIVE
LIGUORI MO 63057-9999

Imprimi Potest:
Richard Thibodeau, C.SS.R.
Provincial, Denver Province
The Redemptorists

Imprimatur:
Most Reverend Michael J. Sheridan
Auxiliary Bishop, Archdiocese of St. Louis

ISBN 0-7648-0162-7
Library of Congress Catalog Card Number: 97-74320

Scripture quotations are from the *New Revised Standard Version of
the Bible*, copyright © 1989 by the Division of Christian Education
of the National Council of the Churches of Christ in the USA.
Used with permission. All rights reserved.

Cover art used by permission of the Oblates of Mary Immaculate.

To order, call 1-800-325-9521
http://www.liguori.org

Cover design by Christine Kraus

Contents

Introduction

Mary—Blessed Mother—Blessed Virgin—Holy Virgin Mary—Madonna—Mother of God—Notre Dame—Queen—Our Lady! Mary is the woman of all names, all faces, all nations.

All generations and races acknowledge and respect this unique woman. She has been given numerous faces in art, and her image has graced the cover of national magazines and postage stamps around the world. Songs have been dedicated to her, and books have been written about her.

Though we have little historical data about Mary's personality, she stands forth as a potent symbol of what it means to be a true follower of Jesus Christ. No other woman has shed so much light on the history of the world and of the Church. No other woman has been so graced by God.

Mary is as relevant today as she has been throughout the two-thousand-year history of the Church. She is as much a woman of the twenty-first century as she was of the first century; as much at ease in the space age as in ancient Palestine.

Mary understands the challenges confronting us today. As homemaker, mother, housewife, provider, Jew, and disciple, she deals with situations common to anyone in every generation.

"But," you may ask, "would Mary have put Jesus in day

care? Would Mary have taken Jesus to Little League practice? Would Mary have worked outside the home in a career?" These certainly are interesting questions, but they focus on hypothetical issues. What is important is Mary as a woman of faith and strength, someone we can relate with today. She copes with the growing independence of an adolescent; she carries the heavy reality of being a single parent and widow; she feels the heartache of the empty nest syndrome—all situations common to our experiences today, and all part of Mary's "yes" to God's plan.

Mary is no stranger to undue hardship. In response to a government edict shortly before her baby is due, she has to abandon comfortable surroundings to give birth in an unfamiliar environment. She experiences homelessness and is a refugee and a victim of violence. Her Son escapes the rage of Herod, but only at the expense of other innocent lives. Three decades later, she stands at the foot of the cross, grief-stricken and courageous as her Son is crucified.

Truly every generation has called Mary "blessed" because every generation experiences situations with which Mary is most familiar. As a human being chosen for a unique role, Mary stands out as a model and ideal for all of us.

How can we capsulize in this short space all that Mary stands for and means for Catholics today? What is Mary's role in the Church? How have the ages developed devotion to her? How has Marian piety affected the beliefs and spirituality of Catholics?

This present work tries to answer these basic questions and create a clear understanding of Mary's role today, giving her the rightful place in the history of the world and in the history of salvation. Our aim is to instill a reverent respect and love for this woman, this human being, who is so intimate with God.

This work is divided into four parts. Part I begins most fittingly with Mary of the Scriptures. After some simple exploration, the evidence found in Scripture tells us much more about Mary than we might expect. We also consider some aspects of Mary's life as a Jew and look at works written at the same time the gospels were, but which were not considered "inspired."

Part II reviews Church history and traces Mary's effect on the Church throughout each age, bringing us to a better understanding of what Mary means for us today.

Part III discusses various types of devotion to Mary: Mary in the public worship of the Church through liturgy and feast days, Mary in popular devotions such as the rosary, and Mary in our personal prayer life.

Part IV notes Marian prayers, Marian apparitions, Marian shrines, and other interesting Marian facts.

Mary is the exemplar and model of all human beings who strive to discern God's will and live with the contingencies of life, both its joys and sorrows. Although this overview cannot include all of what can be said of Mary, may it be one in a long line of tributes to her, aiding us to become more fervent in our devotion and to see her as truly the "one we all call blessed."

PART I

MARY IN SCRIPTURE AND OTHER SOURCES

…Mary, of whom Jesus was born…

Matthew 1:16

The following references locate Mary in the New Testament:

Infancy Narratives: Matthew 1:18-25; Matthew 2:1-23; Luke 1:26-56; Luke 2:1-52
Marriage Feast at Cana: John 2:1-12
"Is this not Jesus, son of Mary?": Matthew 13:55; Mark 6:3; Luke 4:22; John 6:42
"Whoever does the will of God is my mother…": Matthew 12:46-50; Mark 3:31-35; Luke 8:19-21
"Blessed is the womb which bore you…": Luke 11:27-28
On Calvary: John 19:25-27
At Pentecost: Acts 1:14

The following references offer Mary's words found in the New Testament:

"How can this be?": Luke 1:34
"Let it be with me": Luke 1:38
"My soul magnifies…": Luke 1:46-55
"Child, why have you treated us like this?": Luke 2:48
"They have no wine": John 2:3
"Do whatever he tells…": John 2:5

Mary: A Reflection of Christ's Message and Mission

We know very little of the historical Mary. The Scriptures, our knowledge of Jewish life in the first century, and other written accounts are sparse sources. When we look at Mary in the gospels, we know that she is inextricably connected with the life and mission of Jesus. Although she is mentioned in only a few passages and speaks a mere six times, her presence and her words in the New Testament are enough to provide much fruit for our reflection. Her person is historic, yet she is strikingly symbolic as the one who perfectly exemplifies Christ's message and mission.

We need not search long for Mary's influence and

effect on our faith life today as it flows from Scripture. As we reflect on the gospels, we let Mary challenge us to a deeper love of the Lord and a greater commitment to the mission of Christ.

First, however, we must appreciate the gospels with eyes of faith; we must look to their wisdom as the basis of our spirituality. "The Word becomes flesh" and alive for us only when we allow the Scriptures to speak to us personally, within the story of our own life. For the Scriptures are a mirror through which we see God's love and message reflected to us in our daily life and concerns. Let us not be primarily concerned if the events happened the way they are recorded. Rather, a true biblical mentality lets us ask, "What does that mean? What is this passage telling me right now in my situation?"

And so, it is in this sense that we consider Mary's presence in the New Testament. As we reflect on the Marian passages in the New Testament, we apply them to our own situation, and so we use the present tense throughout this section to respect the living Word of God in and through Scripture and the ongoing influence of Mary in all ages.

Mary: Embodiment and Receptacle of God's Will

Mary appears out of nowhere in the Gospel of Luke: "The virgin's name was Mary" (1:27). An angel bears the divine message that she is most blessed, has found favor with God, and is to be the mother of the Messiah. The Annunciation scene, one of the most loved passages in the gospels, is all too familiar to us because so many artists have portrayed it.

God chooses Mary from all eternity. In Mary, God envisions the perfect creature who is worthy to nurture Jesus' physical being. God knows that the person Mary and what Mary will do are in perfect conformity to God's own divine will. Mary perfectly embodies the woman God chooses as mother. We see all this played out in the gospel as the angel addresses Mary, "Greetings, favored one" (Luke 1:28), and Mary, in turn, accepts God's will and is totally open. She is not, of course, without questioning and discerning: "How can this be...?" (Luke 1:34).

Mary is to be mother, yet remain a virgin: a paradox, indeed. Perplexed and confused is a mild way to describe Mary's innermost feelings. But she is open and asks "How?" Mary is responsive and realizes that when God speaks to the heart, she cannot but listen.

God comes to us not in the dramatic way the angel comes to Mary, but in those deep-felt inspirations, in our quiet, in our listening to the promptings of God's grace within. God calls each of us to a certain task and, like Mary, we are to be conformed to the divine will just as Mary. We, too, need to discern. We, too, need to question. We, too, need to be open for "impossible possibilities" for which only God has the solution.

Mary's Annunciation challenges us to consider our own annunciations. Although no angel speaks to us, God does send those who announce God's will for us. It may be a knock on the door from a needy neighbor; it may be the cry of someone asking us for a favor; it may be the demands and obligations of our job or state of life; it may be the humdrum of our daily tasks urging us to complete what we have begun; it may be a prompting deep in our heart that inspires and guides us. No matter what God asks of us, we need only look to Mary for guidance and the example of doing God's will most perfectly.

Then there are those times when *we* bear annunciations to others, summoning others to what God is asking of them.

Whether we are in the receptive position of Mary or the active annunciation of the angel, we find in the Annunciation scene the ideal toward which to strive. May our attitude be that of Mary: "Here am I, the servant of the Lord; let it be with me according to your word" (Luke 1:38). When God speaks, we have a model for listening: Mary.

Mary: Support and Sharer of the Good News

Mary shares the Good News with her cousin, Elizabeth (Luke 1:39-56). She offers to her cousin, also pregnant, compassionate support. In moments of great joy and overwhelming grief, we need someone with whom to share, and that's what Mary does as she shares her divine secret with Elizabeth. She not only shares her own concerns, but she cares about Elizabeth and wants to be of assistance. Like a faithful Jew, Mary is convinced that all good things come from the Lord and, living that faith, she pours out her heart in praise: "My soul magnifies the Lord, / and my spirit rejoices in God my Savior" (Luke 1:47).

This scene is a model for us as we share our own concerns, extend ourselves, and reach out to others. We are privileged to see in Mary how the good news of God's wonders can be delivered with great joy. To forget ourselves and to think more of others, we simply follow Mary.

God gifts each of us according to divine designs. When some surprise from the Lord comes to us, we have Mary's praise and thanksgiving to make our own. In those quiet moments of grace and those incredible events, we see the "goodness of the Lord" with Mary's eyes of faith. Like Mary, our faith allows us to embrace it all as God's presence—and presents.

Mary: Participating in the Messianic Promise

The birth of Jesus, recorded in both Matthew (1:18-25) and Luke (2:1-20), is the epitome of Christian beliefs. Matthew looks at the birth from Joseph's point of view; Luke zeroes in on Mary's role.

The Christmas story, from either account, is one of the best known and loved Bible stories. During Advent, we can get carried away by the details of the nativity in

16

plays, art, carols, greeting cards, crèches, and the human imagination. Theologians and Scripture scholars, however, have probed the deeper meanings of the event and have offered explanations for understanding the divine mystery of the virgin birth. They see the nativity as the perfect realization of all that Yahweh had promised—with Mary's role being central to the fulfillment of the messianic prophecies of the old law as they come to fruition in the person of Jesus.

Although the scene is simple, its lessons are inexhaustible. Not everyone has the privilege of physical motherhood but, like Mary, we are called to "birth Christ" in this world. How? We birth Christ when we share our faith and love for the gospel. We birth Christ when we tell others about God's grace in our lives. We birth Christ when we spread the Good News of God's love. We birth Christ when we use our creative abilities to keep alive the Christian spirit in the world.

In this age of evangelization, the "birthing of Christ" is as urgent as it has been in every age. As members of the Church, we make Christ visible in the world through authentic Christian witness, living our belief in Jesus Christ as our Messiah.

Mary and Joseph are not above the Law. They present Jesus in the Temple and offer what they can—two turtle doves (Luke 2:22-38). Jesus does not need to be presented; he is the Son of God. Mary does not need to be purified; she is the bearer of God's promise to the world. Yet, this humble family seeks no exemption; they do what the Law requires. Like all young parents, however, Mary and Joseph wonder what will become of their lad when they hear the hard words from Simeon: "This child is destined for the falling and the rising of many in Israel…and a sword will pierce your own soul too" (Luke 2:34,35).

Mary: Bearer of Promise and Prophecy

The Presentation in the Temple sets before us the example of fidelity and respect for the Law. After all, we are all subject to laws in one form or another. Yet, how often we seek the easy way out and cut corners to avoid duties. Easy it is to notice when others shirk responsibility, but it takes a sensitive conscience to see one's own shortcomings.

We're not realistic if we do not respect the fact that life consists of joys and sorrows. Sometimes we get so wrapped up in life's fleeting pleasures that we are not prepared when the hard times hit. Like Mary and Joseph, we hear Simeon's words of caution and faithfully heed his joy: "My eyes have seen your salvation" (Luke 2:30).

Mary: A Woman of Fidelity

To flee to a foreign land: this is Mary's first experience of the sword of which Simeon spoke (Matthew 2:12-23). It is a trip into the unknown, across barren desert, without the basic securities of safe lodging and adequate food. As with the other accounts, we know only bare facts, and it matters not whether the event is historically accurate. The account is an example of what we all experience immersed in the human condition.

Just think of the absolute faith and fidelity Mary and Joseph exhibit as they venture the unknown hazards of foreign terrain and wilderness, and their own mixed human emotions of fear, loss, and confusion. When we seek the comforts and security of life, when we get upset with minor setbacks, when our television sets flash with the miseries and heartaches of humanity, victims of floods, wars, and violence, we recall these three lonely wanderers. The image of their desperate flight ignites our compassion and sympathy, leaving us ready to take risks, to go the extra mile, to trod an unknown trail—even at the cost of our own security and comfort.

Although the Gospel of Luke tells us nothing of the lifestyle in the home at Nazareth, we can imagine Mary's meticulous care and concern for Son and husband. (See Luke 2:39-40.) In the eyes of the world, Mary does not do great things. Rather, she lives her life doing the mundane tasks of each day, making sacred the simple and the ordinary.

Mary is content to do her best each day, living as a person of faith, fully immersed in the present moment, humble. We watch Mary model for us a spirit and attitude for daily life: commitment to the ordinary.

Mary faces the temptation of being overprotective of Jesus, who goes through all the growing pains and adventures of any young Jewish boy of his day. We watch Mary's frustration at Jesus' teenage independence when he stays behind in Jerusalem (Luke 2:41-52). Mary's words, "Child, why have you treated us like this?" mirror the sentiments of a distraught mother wondering exactly what it is her child needs from her.

Like any mother, Mary wholeheartedly devotes herself to her mission of caring for her child—a child she knows is special—and treasures "all these things in her heart." In wonder, she watches Jesus grow, not fully realizing all that her simple and quiet life entails as that child's mother.

Day in and day out, Mary lives with the "promised Messiah." What faith! Imagine her spending sleepless nights trying to fathom the mystery of God in her life and how Yahweh would ultimately fulfill the divine plan she could only glimpse when the angel first brought her the news so many years earlier.

When we are perplexed and confused with what the Lord expects of us, we need only think of Mary and her faithful devotion, living quietly and contemplatively with the responsibility of the salvation of the world under

Mary: Extraordinary Commitment in Ordinary Tasks

Mary: Caring Mother and Ponderer of Mystery

her roof. When we are faced with life's responsibilities—hardly as weighty as the salvation of the world—we have Mary's faith to lead the way. Like Mary, we can let go of attachments by living simply. When it seems we must let go of more than we can possibly release, we remember Mary then, too, totally surrendering to her God, carrying the mission of "mother"—nothing more, nothing less. When we find ourselves attached to that which is impermanent, Mary teaches us the art of letting go so we can ponder the mystery of God.

Mary: Hostess and Perfect Guest

Concerned to preserve the dignity of the young couple and not wishing for them to be embarrassed by running out of beverages, Mary tactfully intervenes at the wedding feast in Cana (John 2:1-12). "They have no wine," she tells her Son, knowing he can do something about it. With motherly care and feminine intuition she directs the waiters, "Do whatever Jesus tells you."

Should we then hesitate to call on her when things are in need of being mended in our lives? Does our faith allow us to believe she still intervenes on our behalf? Do we believe that Mary looks after each of us in a maternal way? Most of all, do we call on Mary, knowing her intimacy with her Son allows her to direct others to "do as he says"?

Mary: Listener and Personification of God's Will

Mary is a bystander and faithful disciple in Jesus' public life. Rather than demanding recognition for her role of "mother," she simply loves her Son from a humble and quiet distance. In one scene, for example, we see Jesus speaking to a group of disciples who note, "Your mother…[is] outside asking for you" (Mark 3:32). Jesus responds, "Here [is] my mother….Whoever does the will of God is…my mother" (Mark 3:34-35). Mary willingly takes a back seat in Jesus' public ministry.

In another scene, we hear a woman in the crowd cry

out with a blessing for Jesus' mother: "Blessed is the womb that bore you," and again we hear Jesus respond: "Blessed rather are those who hear the word of God and obey it!" (Luke 11:27-28).

Jesus is not demeaning his mother in either of these scenes. Rather, he is upholding her as the paradigm and exemplar of all those who do God's will in all things. Mary's care and concern continue as she follows her Son's mission in her quiet and unassuming way.

Mary shows us how to prioritize the details of life, always pursuing the will of God, with no personal gain in mind.

The Gospel of John mentions Mary "standing near the cross" at Jesus' crucifixion. From the cross, Jesus addresses his mother, "Woman, here is your son," and John, "Here is your mother," placing the two together in a bond of mutual care (John 19:25-27). Certainly, we see arrangements here for Mary's physical well-being. But there's much more; Mary steps in and becomes the harbinger and bearer of the message of salvation. As she brought Christ into the world, she stands at the foot of the cross and "births" the community that will continue his mission. Mary becomes the mother of all those who follow Christ, serving as a stalwart model of courage and faith.

Mary: Bearer of Her Cross in Suffering

Mary bears one of life's harshest sufferings—the violent death of her child. Yet, under the brutal weight of her grief she continues in her mission. For it is up to her to "mother" the early community of Christians, to nurture its faith. There, at the foot of the cross, helpless and brokenhearted, she truly becomes the Mother of the Church.

Weeping with this woman of sorrow, we ask, "To what degree do I emulate this kind of valor? Do I stand by faithfully when hardship comes or am I like those who run away? When life gets too hard, when life's burdens seem unbearable, am I willing to go to the cross and draw strength from the silent fidelity and presence of Mary? When my own crosses become 'crucifixions' for me, can I turn to Mary and ask for the same calm, loving, caring presence she took to Calvary?"

Mary: Active Presence Among the Early Christians

In just a few words, the Acts of the Apostles alludes to Mary's presence at Pentecost. The Apostles are "constantly devoting themselves to prayer...including Mary the mother of Jesus" (1:14).

Mary's presence is no passive attendance veiled with self-pity and lonely sorrow. Rather, Mary's presence energizes; she is a potent catalyst that prompts the disciples to fearlessly proclaim "Jesus is alive." Mary witnesses to her belief in Jesus' Resurrection and participates in ardent prayer to affirm her mission as "Mother of the Church."

Mary's life after the Pentecost experience is not recorded, but we can imagine she continues to encourage the apostles and disciples to walk in the "way" Jesus taught and to take over where Jesus left off. Today, Mary continues to point the "way" to Jesus. By our baptism we take on an active presence in the mission of the Church. It's not merely a membership card we carry in our wallet stating "I am a baptized Christian." Rather, our commitment at baptism demands we take and assume responsibility for spreading the gospel. Making visible the kingdom of God is not only the prerogative of the "professionals" in the Church, but is the mission of all the baptized. With the balm and hope of our Christian faith, we counteract the evils and violence so rampant in our day. "Being there" means bringing an active presence into the work of Christ. Mary points the way.

Mary is an especially strong model for all nonordained ministers within the Church. In our day when there is a need for laity to become more involved in the work of the Church, Mary is the paragon of lay involvement and influence. As the Church depends more and more on the laity's responsibility for carrying out the Church's mission, Mary stands forth as model and patroness.

Mary's presence in the New Testament is enough to portray the unique role she plays within the Christian faith today. In the Scriptures, she seems to appear abruptly and then quietly fades in words we never hear. Yet, her spirit and example stand out as the embodiment of all the ideals Jesus taught. We need go no further than to Mary of the gospels to know what it means to be a perfect follower of Christ.

True, Scripture says little, but what it does record is enough for us to realize that Mary is a key figure in the New Testament and the early Church. Her impact continues today, within the Church around the world.

Mary in Apocryphal Writings

The New Testament does not include many "behind-the-scenes" details we would like to know about Mary and the life of the Holy Family. Even the gospels do not totally satisfy our human curiosity because they are primarily testimonies of faith of the early Christian community; they deal with material significant to the message and mission of Jesus, not with minute details.

We humans tend to fill in the gaps, however. So, too, did storytellers of the first century. With their creative imaginations, they compiled fanciful anecdotes that included facts not specifically mentioned in the Scriptures.

This body of literature, known by Catholics as the "apocryphal books," was woven around significant events or persons in Scripture. Similar to the supermarket tabloids of today, this literature fed popular curiosity and chronicled tales of an intimate and private nature.

As many as forty apocryphal works were circulated among the early Christians from about the middle of the second century to the fifth century. The apocryphals, although they contained material based on gospel facts, primarily recorded legendary, sometimes outlandish, details. Nonetheless, several of these works give us a glimpse of Mary's private life and personality, and deserve mention here.

A work known as the Protoevangelium of James, for example, relates details of Mary's childhood. Purportedly written by the apostle James, the Less, and circulated around A.D. 150, it named Mary's parents, described her service in the Temple as a virgin from the age of three, and chronicled her giving birth to Jesus in a cave. Joseph is described as an elderly widower with several children from a previous marriage. This answers the oft-raised question about whether Jesus had brothers and sisters.

Another work, the Gospel of Thomas, depicted Jesus as a precocious lad who used his divine powers to work miracles. A behind-the-scenes look into the Holy Family's sojourn into Egypt and the names of the three Magi are recorded in another work called the Arabian Gospel of the Infancy. Mary's behavior on Calvary as hysterically grief-stricken is related in the Gospel of Nicodemus.

Although the apocryphals were popular among the people, the official Church looked on them with caution. As a result, the Gelasian Decree in the fifth century ordered that only the approved Scriptures be read in public worship.

The apocryphals were not totally rejected by the Church, however. Two specific items in the apocrypha have been incorporated into the Church's tradition and liturgy. The names of Mary's parents, Anne and Joachim, recorded in the apocryphal Gospel of James are honored in the liturgy on July 26, and Mary's Presentation in the Temple at the age of three, recorded in the same gospel, is commemorated in the liturgy on November 21.

The apocryphals did not contain fabricated material; rather they added fanciful detail to already existing traditions. For example, the Passing of Mary, which details Mary's later years and her death, was penned after belief in her Assumption was an established tradition.

The apocryphals regained popularity in the Middle Ages when questions about the hidden life of Jesus were raised and theologians centered on the human life of Christ. Classical religious medieval art, devotions, and piety drew on apocryphal material. Today interest in the apocryphals is increasing because several fragments have been unearthed and translated.

What value, then, do the apocryphals have on Christian beliefs? Although they have no authoritative status, they provide insights into the mentality of the early Christians' efforts to answer theological questions through creative storytelling. They also contain some nuggets of truth as well as uplifting inspiration. We cannot forget that the early Christian community, imbued with knowledge of the prophecies, attemped to totally harmonize the prophecies with real life. The apocryphals, while they may be thought-provoking, inspiring, and interesting, will never attain the degree of truth and reverence of the Scriptures, however.

Mary: Jewish Maiden and Mother

Most Christians need to be aware that Jesus grew up in a Jewish household. As observant Jews, Mary and Joseph lived their daily life in accordance with Jewish laws and customs. Although Mary's lineage could be traced from the royal line of David, she belonged to the *anawim*, the pious remnant who observed the Jewish way of life simply and sincerely. As a woman of faith, longing for the day of the promised Messiah, Mary naturally followed the Lord's promptings in her heart when the angel addressed her. Imagine, if you will, the small-town gossip when Mary was found pregnant. Nevertheless, she accepted the situation in faith and provided a loving and caring environment for Jesus and Joseph.

Jesus was circumcised when he was eight days old, and after forty days, he was presented in the Temple and Mary was purified—all according to Jewish law. Mary and Joseph offered the customary gift of the poor: two turtle-doves. What thoughts and sentiments did Mary and Joseph experience in the midst of all this? Their deep faith and Simeon's prophecy assured them that their child was special.

The Letter of Paul to the Philippians tells us that Jesus emptied himself of his divinity (2:7) and so needed to learn the human things about growing up. The gospels give us no particulars other than that he lived in Nazareth, was obedient to Mary and Joseph, and increased "in wisdom and in years" (Luke 2:52). Since early training falls to the mother, it is safe to assume that Mary schooled Jesus in basic human behaviors and the Jewish way of life.

Although it was the duty of the men to pray thrice daily, Mary, too, focused herself in prayer as she treasured "all these things in her heart" (Luke 2:51). According to Jewish custom, each time Mary felt divine aid or saw a thing of beauty she raised a blessing with the *B'rakah*: "Blessed are you Lord, God, King of the universe." That is how pious Jews kept the presence of God alive in their daily lives.

As a typical Jewish wife and mother, Mary went about her daily tasks of cooking, sewing, and caring for the details of her family's home, aware of God's presence and Yahweh's Messiah in her care. One wonders what she thought as she quietly sewed the tassels on Joseph's prayer shawl and the shawl Jesus would wear on his first trek to the Temple at the age of twelve for his *Bar Mitzvah*.

Mary strolled daily to the village well to draw water for household use. To this day, that well is a hallowed spot in Nazareth.

Each Friday, Mary no doubt cleaned, washed, cooked,

and filled the lamps with oil in preparation for the Sabbath. Mary lit the candles on Sabbath evening while Joseph recited the traits of the perfect wife from Proverbs 31.

Each week, the Holy Family went to the synagogue at Nazareth, joining friends and family along the way, to observe the Sabbath. Mary, like all Jewish women, took her place with the other women as the men prayed in a separate space.

From the gospels we know that Jesus, Mary, and Joseph celebrated the Jewish feasts and made pilgrimages to Jerusalem several times a year. We know that twelve-year-old Jesus remained behind in the Temple on one of these trips. We also know that Jesus was "about thirty years old" when he began his public ministry (Luke 3:23) and that Mary's faith in God was remarkably strong as she bid farewell to her Son. She knew the hostile world her Son was entering, and she bravely faced the "empty nest syndrome."

But Mary's work was far from complete when Jesus started his public ministry. As a faith-filled Jew, Mary lived the prophecies foretold of her Son. At the foot of the cross and in the upper room, Mary exemplified the faithful Jew, the New Eve, the New Ark of the Covenant. Mary, the human vessel through whom God entered our humble world, steadfastly anticipated the fulfillment of God's promises in the Resurrection and awaited the outpouring of the Spirit her Son promised.

Conclusion

Through Mary, the Son of God came to proclaim the Good News. Through Mary's life and example, the People of God continue her mission.

No matter what our status or role in life, no matter what niche we fill in the world, Mary has something to offer us—her own life and attitude. Mary, like the Lord, is with us always.

Her role as Mother of the Church assures us that faith in her Son will endure in spite of setbacks and hardships. Mary, who guided Christ in his earthly life, will be no less effective in continuing her guidance and inspiration in our lives. We just need to ask her.

PART II

MARY THROUGH THE AGES

*…from now on all generations
will call me blessed…*

Luke 1:48

L ike Jesus who promised "I am with you always," Mary remains in the hearts of believers as an indispensable link of different ages, nations, cultures, and mindsets. As we journey through each age of the Church, we experience the unfolding of a grand mosaic of Mary. We see how Mary assumes the face of each age and lovingly respects the image and devotion each age proffers.

In our generation we benefit from the rich legacy of each age, which has imprinted Mary with its own uniqueness in a variety of ways: in its theological understanding, in its pious practices, in its art and architecture, in its cultural and ethnic customs, and in its ecclesiastical pronouncements and dogmas. In liturgical worship, prayers, devotions, and titles, Mary has acquiesced to our limited human endearments and love.

Mary: A Grand Mosaic

We have no accurate information about Mary's later years or her death. According to tradition and the apocryphal Passing of Mary, she lived out her life as a respected member of the Ephesus community under the care of John the Apostle. In Ephesus today, one can visit the site where Mary supposedly lived. (Another tradition claims Mary died in Jerusalem, where the Church of the Dormition stands today.) The Christian message barely got off the ground, however, when the Roman Persecutions forced Christians underground because of their commitment to Jesus.

Many who followed Jesus died for the faith. These martyrs became most honored and esteemed Christians, their tombs in the catacombs were revered, and their names were recalled in worship services. For these reasons, the Church in the first two centuries showed no signs of special devotion or attention to Mary.

Implicitly, however, Mary's example affected early Christians. Bands of ascetics, wending their way into the desert wilderness, for example, modeled their lifestyle on

The Early Church: A.D. 100-500

Mary's humility and contemplative spirit by their detachment from the world. Patristic writers, such as Justin and Irenaeus, wrote treatises on Mary as the New Eve and used Hebrew scriptural images to explain Mary's role. We still find images of Mary and the child Jesus on the walls of the catacombs. Even some of the primitive baptismal creeds make reference to Mary in their affirmations of belief in Jesus who "was born of the Holy Spirit and of the virgin Mary." The Nicene Creed, formulated in 325, simply states that Jesus was "born of the Virgin Mary." Liturgical manuscript fragments and an ancient prayer ("We fly to your patronage...") invoking Mary's aid date from the fourth century.

Eventually, however, interest in Mary escalated, especially during the fifth century when theologians began questioning the nature of Jesus. This necessarily broached the question of Mary as "mother." Was Mary the mother of Jesus' human nature or, because Jesus was also God, is Mary also the Mother of God? Differences of opinions led to theological controversies and even heresies.

The Council of Ephesus in 431 resolved the issue, declaring Jesus to be God, a divine person possessing two distinct natures, divine and human. Because Mary gave birth to Jesus who is God, Mary logically is the *Theotokos*, "Mother of God."

The pronouncement of this dogma was a theological milestone, and Mary gained a highly respected profile in the Church. Marian feasts were established, Mary was mentioned in every liturgy, and churches were named after her. Saint Mary Major in Rome, built in the fifth century, is today the largest church in Mary's honor. The apocryphal works, of course, with many nonscriptural legends, gradually lost their popular appeal when Pope Gelasius in 495 decreed that only the Scriptures are to be read in public liturgy, but devotion to Mary did not suffer as a result.

Thus for the first five hundred years, Mary, Mother of God, exemplified the perfect disciple and Christian.

Although the years between 600 and 1000 are generally called the "Dark Ages," significant strides in Marian understanding took place. Liturgical reforms of the time, for example, brought the majesty of the Byzantine East and the Roman imperial courts into Western liturgical worship, and thus Mary—*Theotokos*, "Mother of God"—was honored as queen and pictured seated on a throne. With time, an increased popularity and belief in Mary's Assumption and her intimacy with Jesus in heaven led believers to consider Mary to be a powerful mediator. This was carried to such a degree that God was seen as a wrathful judge who forgives only when Mary intercedes. Mary was invoked as "Refuge of Sinners" and "Mediatrix of all Graces." By 600, five Marian feasts were generally observed: Mary, Mother of God (January 1); Mary's Birthday (September 8); the Annunciation (March 25); the Presentation of Jesus in the Temple (February 2); and the Assumption or Dormition of Mary (August 15).

The Dark Ages: 600-1000

A brilliant light of the Dark Ages, Charlemagne, the Holy Roman emperor (800), not only unified the Empire, but left a significant legacy for Christian posterity. He initiated an intrepid crusade to foster learning and theological understanding, bringing together Byzantine, Germanic, and Celtic art forms and thought.

Charlemagne, with a passion for the Church and a desire to preserve our heritage, is credited for safeguarding ancient Marian material from the early days of the Church. The dedication of Saturdays to Mary, for example, was started by Alcuin, Charlemagne's mentor, proving that Mary was highly revered during this time.

After the East separated from the West in 1094, forming the Orthodox Church, the religious spirit in the

The Middle Ages: 1100-1200

West was kept alive in the many monasteries that mushroomed over the countryside. Within these communities, the monks looked to Mary for spiritual inspiration and meticulously preserved her heritage in artfully executed manuscripts. The fruit is a treasured body of Marian literature—treatises, sermons, prayers, liturgical offices, Masses, public proclamations—many of which are extant today.

Bernard of Clairvaux (1153) stands out as the most eloquent proponent of Marian devotion of the twelfth century. Bernard, convinced that Mary is the conduit through whom Christ's redemptive graces come, summed up his sentiments in this way: "If you fear the Father, go to the Son; if you fear the Son, go to Mary, his mother." His sermons "In Praise of Mary" were so powerful and simple that they influenced both the learned and the commonfolk. Bernard traditionally is given credit for the Memorare ("Remember, O most gracious virgin Mary…"), a favorite Marian prayer many of us learned in our religious training as children. Although Bernard had difficulty understanding the Immaculate Conception, he remained a fervent devotee of Mary, as represented most eloquently by Dante in *The Divine Comedy*.

Mary was dutifully honored in this age, as we have seen, but the golden age of Mary was about to dawn.

The Middle Ages and Renaissance: 1300-1500

We cannot fully appreciate nor assess the enormous contribution of the Middle Ages to Marian devotion unless we step into the mindset of that age: a world particularly creative and open to things spiritual.

Imagine you are an ordinary peasant in the Middle Ages. Religion is part and parcel of your life. The Church, as a unifying force, governs all aspects of your life. Everything you do is regulated by religious motives. You look forward to Sundays and liturgical feasts as respite from humdrum daily routines.

As a devout believer, you attend Mass but you feel somewhat like an outsider; you know very little of what's going on and rarely if ever partake of holy Communion. The clergy are the educated ones, so you learn about your religion from sermons.

When the Black Plague (1347-1349) sweeps across your small part of the world, a large segment of the population dies, including members of your own family. As a result, you become preoccupied with death and the afterlife. You seek assurance of your salvation through pious works and deeds. Your prayer life focuses on God's protection. With suffering so rampant, you are influenced by the theology of the time, which emphasizes the humanity of Christ and his sufferings. Sermons help you reflect on the human side of Christ and portray Mary as a tender and caring mother.

But all is not doom and gloom for you. From the Crusaders, you learn of different cultures and outlooks. Explorations increase your awareness of other lands and broaden your knowledge of the world. The Renaissance encourages your self-expression and creativity. You may find yourself among the many artisans who put their talent to work and produce classic masterpieces of art, architecture, and learning. The age of chivalry encourages respect for women, and so naturally you turn your attention more to Mary. Finally, the invention of the printing press revolutionizes communication methods and promotes literacy. Now treatises, books, sermons, hymns, and canticles are preserved and circulated.

Many other currents of history contribute to the religious thinking of the times and ultimately influence your faith and love of Mary:

Mendicant orders: The monks in monasteries keep alive the Christian spirit but, withdrawn and cloistered from the world, they do not directly influence your life. Then

along comes Francis from Assisi (1182-1226), a humble man of God who, in a brown robe and sandals, brings a message of joy, peace, and enthusiasm for God's Word. He attracts many who follow him (Franciscans) who go from town to town begging for food and spreading the tender love of God and Mary. Francis shows special love for Mary, naming his little chapel in Assisi, Mary of the Angels. Francis, aware of the humanness of Jesus, portrays the humanity of Jesus through a live nativity. Thus the Christmas crèche becomes a way to represent the harsh conditions Jesus endured and the great love Jesus showed in his coming to earth. From Francis you learn how joyful it is to serve the Lord.

You also meet up with white-robed friars who roam the streets of towns and villages teaching and preaching. This Order of Preachers, led by Dominic, helps you pray with the rosary—strings of beads or pebbles that help you keep count of your prayers while you think of the stories of Jesus and Mary. The rosary appeals to you because it provides you with an intimate prayer form. Instead of idly looking on during Mass now, you often pray the rosary.

These mendicant friars—the Franciscans and the Dominicans—beg for their food and in turn bring God's word and love of Mary to you directly through their teaching and apostolic witness.

Theologians: Educated friars and theologians devote themselves to study and attempt to put the divine mysteries into human words for you to understand. They raise questions about Christ's human nature and thus pay increased attention to Mary's role. Albert the Great, Thomas Aquinas, Bonaventure, and Duns Scotus pioneer theological inquiry at this time.

In his *Summa*, Thomas Aquinas treats Mary in connection with Christ. He cannot reconcile Mary's freedom from all sin with the teaching on redemption. In this he differs from Duns Scotus, who has no difficulty explaining and believing in the Immaculate Conception. But differing theological abstractions and sophisticated theology have little bearing on your faith during this time. You seek spiritual strength in tangible expressions of faith and especially in your love for Mary.

Mystics: From time to time, you listen to stories of holy persons who have revelations and visions of Mary's life. Among your favorite mystics is Saint Brigid of Sweden, whose visions add to your understanding of Mary.

Art and creative imagination: Along with others, you often wonder what Mary looked like. As a result the creative imaginations of artists of the time offer you images of Mary as they imagine her to have looked. They paint beautiful pictures of Mary with familiar backgrounds, as if Mary is in your backyard. By looking at these portraits you feel in direct communication with the Mother of God. Each tries to put the human imagination to work to present Mary in the most pleasing way, usually interacting with Jesus in some way. Through realistic art, Mary seems close to you, easy to talk to, easy to relate with.

Miracle plays: As a peasant in the Middle Ages you have little opportunity to learn to read. Literacy is the reserve of the privileged classes. But at the same time, your pious ambitions simply are not satisfied by looking at or contemplating art.

Thus, you seek more involvement to express your love for Mary and to make your faith tangible. You attend and participate in miracle plays: stories from the Scriptures acted out by human beings. These help you learn more about your faith and experience a measure of inspiration.

Cathedrals: One day you hear about the great cathedrals that are being built in many of the large cities of your day. You're told that the people's simple faith shouts forth its love in the impressive stone structures. So, you journey as a pilgrim to one of the massive cathedrals built in honor of Mary: Notre Dame in Paris or the Chartres Cathedral in Chartres, for example. You stare upward and are dwarfed by the mighty Gothic spires that seem like humongous praying hands reaching up to the heavens.

As you pass through the gigantic doors of the cathedral, you are confronted by colossal walls and flying buttresses that transport you to a world beyond. "Be still; sense the presence of God" you tell yourself. Like an antechamber to the heavens, a tranquillity floods your being as you stand silent, transfixed by the majestic divine presence.

You are blinded by the brilliance of the wondrous images shining through the multicolored stained glass windows. You recognize scenes from stories you've heard about Jesus, Mary, and the saints. The figures seem so alive in the translucent glow of natural light pouring through the panes. These windows are "the Bible of the poor," for the Word of God takes on flesh in these stained glass windows.

Surrounded by this profound art and faith, you immerse yourself in the mystery of God. Strange, how your fears of death and the afterlife melt into an ardent longing for God. As you touch the cold stones, you recall the words of the psalmist, "God is my rock." You wonder how much human sweat and tears went into the building of this massive structure by thousands of craftsmen, artisans, and laborers who spent many years conscientiously placing stone upon stone.

Words do not come easily, for you are overcome with beauty. Like Peter at the Transfiguration, you pray, "Lord it is so good to be here." You leave with your heart over-flowing with awe. "Surely the presence of the Lord is in this place" is the anthem you carry in your heart.

You cling to a certain reassurance of God's providence and Mary's maternal protection as a result of having visited this holy place. You're not surprised, then, when the Church begins to encourage the faith by granting indulgences—remission of temporal punishment due to sin—to those who pilgrim to the cathedrals.

Though meant to be a living faith experience, however, cathedrals gradually become occasions for exaggerated Marian piety. Carried away with fervor and the desire to allure pilgrims, cities vie with one another and boast of their cathedrals' sacred treasures. Some claim relics of Mary's hair, parts of her tunic, and other articles supposedly used by Mary.

Through it all, you know that the cathedrals will endure as impressive monuments of faith and lasting tributes to Mary.

Poetry and literature: Words have an innate power to transform and convey the heart's deepest emotions. Poets, mystics, and saints create verbal images in poetry, anthems, and canticles as legacies in praise of Mary. You find one of the most inspiring literary tributes to Mary in Dante's *The Divine Comedy*. In the final canto of the "Paradiso" (xxxiii:1-40), as Dante prepares to experience the beatific vision, Bernard of Clairvaux pleads with Mary on behalf of Dante—a prayer that crystallizes the Marian theology of your time.

Another poet, Chaucer, reflects the medieval devotion to Mary through the nun's tale in his classic *Canterbury Tales*.

Popular piety, theological speculation, artistic and architectural creations, scholarly writings, mystical experiences: all these expressions are woven into the rich tapestry of medieval Marian spirituality. The legacy to Mary left by the Middle Ages is a priceless treasure.

Reformation and Counter-Reformation: 1500-1600

But life in the Middle Ages was not perfect. Animosity and prejudice toward the Church increased because of scandals and lack of integrity among the clergy, the selling of indulgences, and outlandish pious practices. So we need not be surprised by the intense reactions of the Reformation. Although the Protestant Reformation challenged and attacked many traditional Catholic beliefs and practices, they did not totally reject Mary.

Martin Luther and John Calvin honored Mary, but they limited their admiration to Mary in Scripture. All other pious devotions and practices honoring Mary and the saints were considered encroachments on Jesus, the only mediator. Luther and Calvin unequivocally denied all pious expressions of the previous ages. As a result of this stance, the role of Mary within the theology of the Church became a caustic bone of contention in the post-Reformation era. Some Protestants, even today, believe Catholics deify Mary.

The Council of Trent (1545-1563), the Catholic Counter-Reformation, defended the Church's stance and upheld devotions in honor of Mary. Although the Council strongly discouraged exaggerated pious practices, controversy continued and forms of Marian piety veered out in other directions. The Sodality, a lay association devoted to spreading Marian piety and good works, was founded by the Jesuits in 1563 and paved the way for Marian organizations and similar confraternities. In 1571, when Muslims were mustering their troops against Christians, Don Juan of Austria faced the stronger Muslim forces and won an overwhelming victory at

Lepanto. In thanksgiving, Pius V, who had urged rosary devotions for the impending onslaught, established the feast of the Holy Rosary: October 7.

The post-Reformation period concentrated on preserving tradition through exacting rituals and laws. It left little room for creative imagination and emphasized orthodoxy in faith and practice. As a result, mariology became a separate branch of theology.

In spite of the efforts of the Enlightenment and the French Revolution to squelch religion and spirituality, Catholicism held its own. The seventeenth century, for example, witnessed a burgeoning of Marian devotions, especially in France and Spain, where Catholicism was a driving force. Missionary orders mushroomed and many named their newfound apostolic organizations in honor of Mary, often developing new titles for her. Saint Louis de Montfort (1673-1716), for example, founded the Missionaries of the Company of Mary and ardently preached a total dedication to Mary. Saint Alphonsus Liguori, founder of the Redemptorists, became noted for his devotion to Mary, especially his tribute to Mary in the classic *The Glories of Mary* (1750). Saint John Eudes propagated devotion to the Immaculate Heart of Mary. In 1878, Father Jules Chevalier founded the Missionaries of the Sacred Heart in Issoudun, France, and put his band of missionaries under the banner of Our Lady of the Sacred Heart.

Post-Reformation: 1600-1800

It is interesting to note that devotion to Mary in the nineteenth century did not originate solely from the common folk, like the piety in the Middle Ages. Rather, the Church hierarchy exerted a powerful leadership in Marian spirituality. To give impetus to Marian piety and to authenticate an already long-held belief, for example, Pope Pius IX declared the dogma of the Immaculate Conception in 1854: "by a special grace of God, Mary was preserved from original sin from the moment of her conception." This belief, though deeply rooted in the early Church, was never defined as dogma.

Just as the Church declared the dogma of the Immaculate Conception, apparitions and visions increased, intensifying Marian devotion. Mary appeared in France, at Paris in 1830, at Lourdes in 1858, and at La Salette in 1846, and at Knock, Ireland in 1879. In fact, each country developed its own unique Marian spirituality. Small wonder the United States is a smorgasbord of Marian devotions, considering the hundreds of thousands of European immigrants who brought along with them their ethnic customs, cultural expressions, and devotions to Mary.

***Modern Era:
1900-***

And so Mary stepped into the twentieth century bedecked with the love of nineteen hundred years of Christian admiration and devotions. The modern world continues to revere and respect Mary—but in quite different ways. Marian devotion remains very much a part of Catholic piety in our present age.

Every pope of the twentieth century has encouraged Marian piety in their encyclicals and letters. The number of lay associations such as the Sodality, Legion of Mary, leagues of prayer, and confraternities devoted to Mary's attributes or titles have increased. In 1917, the apparitions of the Blessed Virgin at Fatima, Portugal strengthened the awareness of Mary's presence and influenced twentieth century Marian devotions. Devotion to Mary's Immaculate Heart and interest in Fatima expanded with the promise of a "secret" which was to have been revealed in 1960. (To date no authoritative or definitive pronouncement has been released.)

Although many persons spread devotion to Mary, two advocates deserve special mention. Father Patrick Peyton (1901-1995), a Holy Cross priest, made it his life's ministry to encourage Marian piety through the family rosary. "The family that prays together, stays together," the motto of his Family Rosary Crusade, was publicized through radio, television, and personal missions.

Another influential preacher and writer, Bishop Fulton Sheen (1895-1979), also advanced devotion to Mary through his popular television series and his bestseller, *World's First Love*.

The highlight of Marian events took place in the 1950 Holy Year when Pope Pius XII proclaimed the dogma of Mary's Assumption on November 1, 1950. This was no spur-of-the-moment decision. Because of increased fervor with the proclamation of the dogma of the Immaculate Conception, millions requested Rome to proclaim the Assumption as dogma. Thus, Pope Pius XII, on the Feast of All Saints, November 1, in the Holy Year 1950, infallibly declared that Mary was taken up body and soul into heaven after her earthly life. The proclamation of the dogma of Mary's Assumption, while not containing details of Mary's death, brought full circle the Church's teaching on Mary: intimately connected in life, Mary and Jesus are fully bonded in eternity, glorified together.

Another significant event in Marian spirituality was the proclamation of 1954 as a Marian Year, the centenary of the definition of the Immaculate Conception.

A Chronological Overview of Dogmas

325: Mary's virginity (Nicene Creed)
431: Mary, the Mother of God (Theotokos)
1854: The Immaculate Conception (Mary is free from original sin)
1950: The Assumption (Mary is assumed into heaven)

Marian Piety Prior to the Second Vatican Council

If you are old enough to remember the days before the Second Vatican Council, you have probably taken part in many forms of Marian devotions. Do you remember, for example, being invested with the Brown Scapular on your first Communion day? reciting the rosary and wondering what mysteries to say on what day? vying to be May Queen, to crown Mary's statue during the May Procession? gathering violets and lilies of the valley for the May altar in your bedroom or classroom? learning the Memorare and other "Mary" prayers? saying the Angelus as the church bells pealed? wearing a medal adorned with a blue ribbon in Mary's months of May and October? saving your blue dresses to wear on Mary's feasts? being one of the "beads" in a living rosary? lighting candles before Mary's altar? collecting Mary holy cards? building a Marian grotto in your yard? going to Mass on first Saturdays? belonging to "the Sodality"? joining a confraternity of prayer or the Legion of Mary? putting Mary's statue on the window sill for good weather on a picnic day? singing "Mother at Your Feet Is Kneeling" while a bride placed a bouquet on Mary's altar? being told that if a girl whistles, Mary cries? burning a vigil light before Mary's statue in church? placing JMJ (Jesus, Mary, Joseph) atop assignments indicating your dedication to the Holy Family and your prayer for a good grade?

As we look over Marian devotions before Vatican II, we see externals: we see the things we *did*. We honored Mary for herself and her virtues, having forgotten somewhere along the line that Mary is intimately connected with Jesus, the Church, and the mysteries of salvation. Although our expressions were devout, laden with a deep faith and sincere spirit, it seems that love of Mary had precedence and overshadowed our worship of God. It's easy to see how some of our Protestant friends got the idea that devotion to Mary was the most important way we practiced our Catholic religion.

The Church Fathers of the Second Vatican Council (1962-1965) revitalized the spirituality of the Church by "reconnecting" us with our ancient traditions and the true spirit of the early Church. Obviously, this has meant major changes in Marian spirituality and devotion.

Vatican II positioned Mary in connection with the mission of the Church and discouraged gross exaggerations in Marian piety. After much discussion and varied opinions, the Council Fathers decided that Mary as Mother of the Church be accorded special treatment in chapter 8 of the Dogmatic Constitution on the Church. This significant decision definitively linked Mary and Marian piety with the central theme of the Scriptures. For the first time in the history of the Church Mary was considered not only an individual graced specially by God but also intimately bonded to the whole Church as a model and ideal.

The Vatican II document considers Mary as unique among God's creatures, chosen and graced by God as the model of holiness which the Church strives to become. The Church looks to Mary as the embodiment of qualities the People of God emulate. The cult or devotion to Mary is secondary to worship of God and Jesus. Mary, a sign of hope for the human family, is the ideal member of the Church.

Has Vatican II done away with Mary? By no means! Rather, Mary has been restored to her rightful place, as model and most faithful disciple of the Church. Private devotions are encouraged as means to personal holiness and aids to one's spirituality.

In 1974, Pope Paul VI clarified and insured a proper balance in Marian spirituality in the apostolic exhortation, *Maria Cultus* (Cult of Mary). It reflects the mind and spirit of Vatican II and sets forth theological principles and practical guidelines so that Marian devotions are in accord with biblical, liturgical, and ecumenical

The Impact of Vatican II on Marian Piety

insights. It exhorts a continued reverence and use of the Angelus and the rosary, but cautions against one-sided or exaggerated notions that could detract from the Church's teachings.

Another significant Marian document is Pope John Paul II's sixth encyclical, *Redemptoris Mater* (Mother of the Redeemer). In preparation for the celebration of the millennium in 2000, the document declares a Marian Year, 1987-1988, and elaborates on contemporary Marian themes such as the mystery of Mary in the plan of salvation, Mary's role as model of the Church, and Mary's mediation. As a synthesis of Marian theology, *Redemptoris Mater* promises to be a classic contribution to post-Vatican II theological thought and one that challenges us today and tomorrow to give due tribute to Mary.

The *Catechism* of the *Catholic* Church

The *Catechism of the Catholic Church*, the recent compendium of Catholic teaching, cites Mary's significance under various headings. The dogmatic teachings about Mary are considered in the article "…Born of the Virgin Mary" (#487-511). Mary's place in the mystery of the Church and the ways she is honored in liturgy and devotion are addressed in "Paragraph 6. Mary—Mother of Christ, Mother of the Church" (#963-975). Mary as the paragon of holiness and perfect model of prayer who leads us to God is considered in Part Four, Christian Prayer (#2030; 2673-2675; 2678-2682). It includes a reflection on the popular Marian prayer, the Hail Mary (#2676-2677).

The above selections are valuable reflections on Mary's role in the Church and her influence in our life.

Conclusion

If we amalgamate the contributions of each age in the development of our understanding of Mary, we find ourselves looking at a kaleidoscope of images, prayers, rituals, and devotions—ways people of all times and all climes have paid and continue to pay tribute to Mary. While these forms of piety have changed from age to age, Mary still wields her maternal influence and care, regardless of one's religious persuasion. Her motherly instinct and love understand the human heart, no matter what form one's expression of piety assumes.

We are challenged always to remember Mary in connection with the Church. In our private prayer we can feel free to utilize any of the rich Marian devotions left to us by previous ages.

PART III

MARY IN LITURGY AND PERSONAL DEVOTIONS

*Pray for us sinners,
now and at the hour of our death…*

Hail Mary

T ake heed of the pulsations of the hearts of the faithful laity, for it is there that the Spirit dwells." This saying, attributed to Saint Paulinus in the third century, has proven prophetic. While dogmas and teachings have come from Church officials, devotions and pious practices have originated with the laity—this includes our affections and devotions for Mary. The people's love for Mary has been expressed in many different ways in each age and culture: Mary, revered as a friend, model, mother, and one to whom we go in times of need.

But true devotion to Mary is always secondary to devotion to the Lord. We do not adore Mary for "latria" adoration, which is given only to God and Jesus. Rather, we honor Mary with the reverence accorded to the saints: "dulia." Because Mary is the most revered of saints, the tribute we give to Mary is called "hyperdulia." Unfortunately, the exaggerated pious practices and attention we Catholics often give to Mary leave those who are not Catholic thinking that we put Mary first, before the Lord. Although devotions to Mary stem from our love and honor of her, our Marian spirituality must be rooted in Mary's close connection with God.

The story is told of an inebriated gent who staggers into Saint Patrick's Cathedral and prays aloud in front of Mary's statue. He begs Mother Mary to get him a good job. A sexton working behind the main altar thinks he can have some fun and so in a booming voice chides, "Yes, Joe, but first you better give up your drinking." The man curtly replies, "Jesus, you be quiet. I'm talking to your mother."

As humorous as this anecdote may be, it portrays the attitude of many Catholics concerning devotion to Mary: go to Mary first before you pray to Jesus. In itself, this simply is not a true portrayal of Mary's role and position in the Church. Most probably, however, all of us at one time or another have been caught up in this mentality.

We Catholics have at our disposal a veritable smorgasbord of Marian devotions. Note that specific devotions honoring a specific aspect of Mary are optional. For example, a person who does not attend a novena in preparation for the Assumption is not denying the dogma, but simply does not wish to participate in a particular prayer form.

In this section we consider Marian devotions in liturgical prayer, official prayer, pious practices, and personal devotions.

Mary in the Liturgy

The primary expression of our Catholic faith lies in the liturgy as our worship of the Lord. Because we believe that those who have attained their eternal reward as members of the communion of saints can intercede for us before the Lord, and because of Mary's singular status in the communion of saints, we honor her through liturgical celebrations and feast days.

Eucharistic prayers: From the earliest days of liturgical celebrations, Mary is included in the main prayer of the Mass: the canon, also called the eucharistic prayer. This part of the liturgy is most solemn and brings before God the intentions and prayers of the whole Church.

Mary is mentioned in each of the four general eucharistic prayers. For example, the first eucharistic prayer reads, "In union with the whole Church, we honor Mary the ever-virgin mother of Jesus Christ, our Lord and God." In the others we pray that "we may be made worthy to share eternal life with Mary, the Virgin Mother of God" or similar words.

Prefaces of the Blessed Virgin Mary: Prefaces in the liturgy serve as introductions to the main part of the Mass and precede the "Holy, Holy, Holy" and the eucharistic prayer. In Masses that honor Mary, there are two prefaces:

one honoring Mary's motherhood and another called "Mary's Song of Praise." The *Sacramentary*, the book used by the celebrant at the altar, also includes prefaces for the Immaculate Conception and the Assumption.

Solemnities, feasts, memorials, votive masses: Throughout the Church year, feasts in honor of Mary occur with regularity, even though liturgical feasts have been diminished in number. The feasts of Mary fall into three categories: solemnities, feasts, and memorials.

The *solemnities* of Mary that commemorate the Marian doctrinal beliefs are celebrated universally and supersede the Sunday liturgies. In the United States these are holy days of obligation: Mary, Mother of God (January 1), the Assumption (August 15), and the Immaculate Conception (December 8).

A fourth solemnity, March 25, is called the "Annunciation of the Lord" in the revised liturgy and not the "Annunciation to Mary," as previously listed. Although March 25 is a solemnity, it is not a holy day of obligation in the United States.

Feasts, though of lesser significance, also are celebrated in the liturgy. In the United States the three feasts include: Mary's Visitation to Elizabeth (May 31), the Birthday of Mary (September 8), and Our Lady of Guadalupe (December 12).

Memorials bring to our attention other titles and events in Mary's life. If no other occasion is being commemorated, the Mass may be that of the memorial. The Marian memorials in the revised liturgy include: Our Lady of Lourdes (February 11), Our Lady of Mount Carmel (July 16), Dedication of Saint Mary Major, Rome (August 5), Mary's Queenship (August 22), Our Lady of Sorrows (September 15), Our Lady of the Rosary (October 7), and the Presentation of Our Lady (November 21).

Other liturgical observances of Mary: Liturgical celebrations in honor of Mary are not restricted to solemnities, feasts, or memorials. On days when there is no other feast, a votive mass in honor of Mary may be celebrated, especially on Saturdays, the day of the week dedicated to Mary.

Although Catholics can choose various ways to honor Mary, joining with the entire Church by observing her feast days is best.

Pious Practices and Personal Devotions

The Catholic faith offers a spectrum of ways to increase one's personal relationship with God and the saints. The following Marian devotions are optional and can be chosen according to one's style of prayer and individual preference.

Angelus: The Angelus is a simple prayer that weaves together the wonder of the Annunciation and the Incarnation. Monks commemorated these mysteries three times a day with the ringing of the monastery bell and the recitation of the prayer known as the Angelus. The bells also summoned the workers from the fields in days before clocks and watches. It is interesting to note that the custom continues in our time; many churches ring their bells at 6:00 a.m, noon, and 6:00 p.m.

Angelus
The angel of the Lord declared unto Mary.
Response: And she conceived of the Holy Spirit. (Hail Mary)

Behold the handmaid of the Lord.
Response: May it be done unto me according to your word. (Hail Mary)

And the Word was made flesh.
Response: And dwelt among us. (Hail Mary)

Pray for us, O holy Mother of God.
Response: That we may be made worthy of the promises of Christ.

Let us pray: O Lord, it was through the message of an angel that we learned of the Incarnation of Christ, your Son. Pour your grace into our hearts, and by his passion and cross bring us to the glory of his Resurrection. Through Christ, our Lord. Amen.

The rosary: The rosary is a meditation/vocal prayer form of devotion focusing on the main mysteries of salvation, using a set of beads.

The rosary as we know it today evolved gradually in the prayer life of the Church. The practice of counting prayers on beads is not uniquely Christian, of course. Hindus, Buddhists, and the lamas of Tibet use prayer beads. The Christian tradition goes back to Irish monks of the eighth century who, in an attempt to simplify prayer for the laity, substituted the Our Father for the one hundred and fifty Psalms. Later, Hail Marys were recited as "Mary's Psalter." Saint Dominic popularized the rosary and it became a common pious practice in the Middle Ages.

The rosary combines vocal prayer with meditation on the scenes from Christ's life called "mysteries." Although there are various ways to pray the rosary, it traditionally is divided into fifteen decades: five Joyful Mysteries, five Sorrowful Mysteries, and five Glorious Mysteries. Each decade consists of an Our Father, ten Hail Marys, and a Prayer of Praise (Glory to the Father...) which are recited while reflecting on one of the mysteries.

Chaplets: Chaplets are variations of the rosary. They are a set of designated prayers repeated on a small set of beads. Many Marian chaplets have appeared over the years honoring Mary and her various titles.

Other forms of prayer: Novenas, public or private prayers repeated nine times for a special intention, constitute another common devotion to Mary. Especially popular are the Immaculate Conception and Miraculous Medal novenas. Other novenas commemorate Mary's various titles.

Litanies, invocations addressed to Mary using her various titles, with the response "Pray for us," are also popular forms of Marian prayer. The Litany of Loreto, the most noted of Marian litanies, is listed as one of the approved litanies of the Church and is used in Marian devotions.

Sacramentals

Sacramentals make ordinary things special by bringing us into contact with the "sacred." Sacramentals are objects, gestures, and blessings that remind us of the sacred and bring us close to God. There are many Marian sacramentals.

Medals: Medals, an ancient sacramental from earliest times, are small coin-like objects used as religious reminders. The catechumens were often given a medal with a cross inscribed on it. Martyrs were commemorated on medals, and when pilgrims visited cathedrals or holy sites during the Middle Ages, they received medals as reminders of the sacred locations.

The Miraculous Medal is perhaps one of the most familiar and popular medals because of the spiritual benefits derived from its use. Its design was revealed by Mary to Saint Catherine Laboure in 1830 and consists of an image of Mary standing on the earth, crushing the serpent's head. Rays of light stream from her outstretched hands, symbolizing graces bestowed through her intercession. The words, "O Mary, conceived without sin, pray for us who have recourse to you," surround her image. On the reverse side are twelve stars, a cross surmounting an "M," and the hearts of Jesus and Mary.

Medals of most Marian devotions and pilgrimage sites are available. Medals in themselves are not amulets and, even if they are blessed, do not carry magical powers. Medals, usually worn around the neck, serve as reminders and excite one to a deeper devotion and faith.

Scapulars: Originally the scapular was part of the monastic religious habit. Gradually, lay associates began wearing scapulars to share in the spiritual benefits of the religious community.

At first the secular scapular consisted of two rectangular pieces of cloth attached by a cord and worn around the shoulders. Today the cloth scapulars can be replaced by medals.

Of the eighteen approved scapulars in the Church, several are devoted to Mary. The Blue Scapular honors Mary as the Immaculate Conception; the White Scapular honors Mary as Our Lady of Good Counsel; the Black Scapular commemorates the Seven Sorrows of Mary.

The most well-known scapular, the Brown Scapular, dates back to Saint Simon Stock, a Carmelite monk who received the scapular from the Blessed Mother in 1251 with the promise that those who wear it will be saved.

The Green Scapular promotes devotion to the Immaculate Heart of Mary. Its origin dates back to 1840, to a vision granted to Sister Justine Bisqueyburu, a Sister of Charity. One side of the scapular pictures Mary showing her Immaculate Heart; the other side contains the prayer, "Immaculate Heart of Mary, pray for us sinners now and at the hour of our death" inscribed around Mary's heart pierced by a sword. The Green Scapular is credited with many miracles, especially bringing people back to the faith.

Images: Images of Mary come in a variety of forms. The most popular are madonnas and Marian masterpieces. Most Catholics have their favorite "images" of Mary.

Over the years, Mary has been pictured in many ways and has been given many faces. It would be accurate to say that Mary is the most multifaced person ever imaged and that her images reflect the times and cultures from which they were generated.

The Marian iconography and art of the Middle Ages, for example, constitutes one of the most prolific bodies of work in Church history. The masterpieces of this time bring out Mary's maternal love and care. Mary is portrayed as a loving madonna in works of Fra Angelico, Murillo, Raphael, Michaelangelo, and others. The image of Mary holding the dead body of Christ, immortalized by Michaelangelo in his *Pieta*, stands forth as one of the best-loved and most famous portrayals of Mary.

Classical madonnas are still popular as subjects on Christmas cards and yuletide postage stamps of many countries.

Icons: We cannot leave this section without noting that the icon has made a significant contribution to Marian piety and art. Icons play a major role in the faith of Eastern Christians.

The familiar two-dimensional images characterized by elongated faces, bold piercing eyes, and disproportionate features symbolize spiritual realities that reach beyond time. Iconography, the art of painting icons, is considered a sacred ministry and the artist prepares with prayer and fasting. A well-known icon revered in Eastern and Western Christianity is the icon of Our Lady of Perpetual Help.

Votive candles or lights: As you enter Catholic churches and pilgrimage sites, you notice candles or lights burning in front of Mary statues. These vigil lights "keeping watch" symbolize our heartfelt prayers that continue to be offered as the candle or light burns. With the ever-present concern for fire safety, many such candles have been replaced with electric bulbs that light when a coin is dropped into a slot. "To light a candle" remains a pious practice to ask for a special favor or intention.

Processions: Processions have always been a popular way to demonstrate devotion and faith. May processions and rosary processions are familiar ways Catholics honor Mary. Many ethnic groups have processions to honor a special title of Mary: for example, the Spanish honor Our Lady of Guadalupe, the Italians honor Our Lady of Mount Carmel, and the Polish honor Our Lady of Czestochowa.

Associations and confraternities of the laity: Throughout the history of the Church, lay persons who wished to devote themselves more closely to a spiritual life and apostolic works formed associations or confraternities distinct from religious communities (no vows). Catholics of pre-Vatican II days, no doubt, remember the Sodality as a vital and active parish organization. Composed mostly of young unmarried women, the Sodality provided a spiritual, apostolic, and social outlet as well as a deeper spiritual life for its members. Devotion to Mary was promoted by recitation of the rosary at meetings and a May procession and crowning of the Blessed Virgin Mary's statue by a chosen "May queen."

The Sodality was started in 1563 by John Leunis, a Jesuit priest, and emphasized Marian devotion, frequent Communion, and personal piety. Because of the renewal of scriptural, liturgical, and ecumenical spirituality that issued from Vatican II, the Sodality is now known as "Christian Life Communities."

The Legion of Mary is another popular lay association. It was organized in Dublin, Ireland, in 1921, by Frank Duff, who was inspired by the devotion of Louis de Montfort. Members of the Legion of Mary attend weekly meetings where they pray together, do spiritual reading, and plan specific apostolic works. Today the Legion of Mary is an active lay movement with millions of advocates in many countries.

Conclusion   We all reach out to God on our own wavelength; we all have our most comfortable and most intimate forms of prayer. Mary fits into our personal prayer life in any form we choose. She listens to us whether we choose a long litany, a persevering novena, or a rosary; whether we wear a medal or reflect on her influence in the Scriptures. Whatever devotion appeals to us and aids us in our own prayer style, Mary is approachable and relevant, regarding only the *spirit* that animates our devotion, not our actions and words.

PART IV

MARY IN PRAYERS, APPARITIONS, AND SHRINES

Mother of Mercy, our life,
our sweetness, our hope.

Salve Regina

Mary has been honored throughout history with many prayers, canticles, hymns, and songs. Although there are myriad forms of prayer to Mary, there are some standard prayers that are universally known.

Blessed Are You Among Women

Hail Mary

Hail Mary, full of grace. The Lord is with thee. Blessed art thou among women, and blessed is the fruit of thy womb, Jesus. Holy Mary, Mother of God, pray for us sinners, now and at the hour of our death. Amen.

This is the most common Marian prayer among Catholics. Called the "Angelic Salutation" and "Ave Maria," it capsulizes most perfectly the role of Mary in the Church. The first part derives from the angel's salutation to Mary (Luke 1:28) and Elizabeth's greeting to Mary (Luke 1:42). The second part, "Holy Mary, Mother of God…" addresses Mary as Mother of God and invokes her intercession. This part of the prayer was added after Mary's divine maternity was declared a dogma at Ephesus in A.D. 431. Later, Saint Peter Damian (1072) testified that the Hail Mary had become a popular prayer of the people, so much so that the Synod Statutes of Paris in 1210, less than two hundred years later, recommended the "Ave Maria" be memorized along with the Our Father and the Creed.

In the Middle Ages the Hail Mary replaced the Psalms as the "poor man's breviary" through devotion to the rosary. The Hail Mary reached its present form in the sixteenth century with the addition of "now and at the hour of our death." As a basic Catholic prayer, the Hail Mary is used in both public and private prayer, especially as part of the rosary and the Angelus.

Memorare

Remember, O most gracious Virgin Mary, that never was it known that anyone who fled to your protection, implored your help, or sought your intercession was left unaided. Inspired with this confidence, I fly to you, O virgin of virgins, my Mother. To you I come, before you I stand, sinful and sorrowful. O Mother of the Word Incarnate, despise not my petitions, but in your mercy, hear and answer me. Amen.

The Memorare is generally attributed to Bernard of Clairvaux (1090-1153), a fervent devotee of Mary. But it was popularized in the seventeenth century by a Frenchman, Father Claude Bernard, who considered Mary a powerful intercessor.

Salve Regina (Hail, Holy Queen)

Hail, holy queen, mother of mercy, our life, our sweetness, our hope. To you we cry, poor banished children of Eve; to you we send up our sighs, mourning and weeping in this valley of tears. Turn, then, O most gracious advocate, your eyes of mercy toward us, and after this our exile, show unto us the blessed fruit of your womb, Jesus. O clement, O loving, O sweet virgin Mary. Pray for us, O holy Mother of God.

Response: *That we may be made worthy of the promises of Christ.*

Let us pray: O God, whose only begotten Son, by his life, death, and Resurrection, has purchased for us the rewards of eternal life, grant, we beseech you, that meditating upon these mysteries of the most holy rosary of the Blessed Virgin Mary, we may imitate what they contain and obtain what they promise. Through the same Christ our Lord. Amen.

The Salve Regina, attributed to Herman Richenau (1054), has been sung in Latin at the Divine Office at the end of the day in monasteries since the Middle Ages. In 1890 Pope Leo XIII ordered the Salve Regina and other prayers to be recited after low masses. This practice lasted until the liturgical renewal of Vatican II in 1964. The Salve Regina is sung or prayed in the Divine Office and in connection with the rosary.

Stabat Mater (At the Cross Her Station Keeping)

At the cross her station keeping,
Stood the mournful mother weeping,
Close to Jesus to the last.

This ancient anthem of many stanzas is used during Lenten devotions; a stanza usually is sung between each station of the cross. From my days in classical literature studies, I recall a "rest of the story" anecdote about the origin of this favorite Lenten hymn.

Jacapone DaTodi, a wealthy worldly lawyer, took his saintly and pious wife to a bullfight at which she was gored to death by a bull. As Jacapone cradled his wife's lifeless body, he saw under her satin-and-lace clothing the hair shirt she wore in penance for his conversion. Distraught and touched, he converted, became a Franciscan monk, and penned mystic poems. His most famous work, the "Stabat Mater," was allegedly written in memory of his wife and dedicated to Mary's sorrows.

We Fly to Your Patronage

We fly to your patronage, O holy Mother of God; despise not our petitions in our necessities but deliver us from all dangers, O ever glorious and Blessed Virgin.

This powerful prayer invoking Mary's aid was thought to be of medieval origin. In 1917, however, a papyrus fragment from the third century A.D. was discovered, on which the prayer was inscribed. As such, it may be the oldest prayer that expresses belief in Mary's power of intercession.

The Magnificat (Luke 1:47-55)

My soul magnifies the Lord,
*   and my spirit rejoices in God my Savior,*
for he has looked with favor on the lowliness of his servant.
*   Surely, from now on all generations will call me blessed.*

For the Mighty One has done great things for me,
  and holy is his name.
His mercy is for those who fear him
  from generation to generation.
He has shown strength with his arm;
  he has scattered the proud in the thoughts of their hearts.
He has brought down the powerful from their thrones,
  and lifted up the lowly;
he has filled the hungry with good things,
  and sent the rich away empty.
He has helped his servant Israel,
  in remembrance of his mercy,
according to the promise he made to our ancestors,
  to Abraham and to his descendants forever.

This canticle, spoken by Mary when she visits her cousin Elizabeth, is recorded in Luke's Gospel. We might think Mary waxes poetic, but her prayer echoes the Hebrew Scripture passage, 1 Samuel 2:1-10. Today this anthem is used in the Divine Office and is sung as a Marian hymn of praise.

Dante's Praise of Mary (a paraphrase of *Paradiso,* xxxiii: 1-39)

Virgin Mary, you are lowly and at the same time full of regal majesty as the apple of Divinity's eye. You are the one through whom the creator did not hesitate to come down to us. The bud of love begotten in you flowered into everlasting peace. In heaven you are the shining splendor of God's love; to us here below you are a vibrant ray of hope. O Mary, glorious and victorious, if we neglect to call on you in our needs, we are like birds without wings. Your maternal concern reaches out even before we call on you, for you are mercy and compassion. In you is the entire goodness of the world compressed. May we be ever secure in your love; look on us as we extend our hands to you in prayer.

A high point in Marian praise comes at the end of *The*

Divine Comedy, as Bernard pleads with Mary on Dante's behalf. This prayer impressed me so much that it is now part of my Marian prayer repertoire.

Since the early days of the Church there have been over eighty thousand reported visions and apparitions of Mary. People have a penchant for unusual supernatural phenomena and will gravitate toward any reported sighting. I recall when people flocked to a tree in a city park because the image looked like Mary. It turned out to be the shadow of a beer bottle from a nearby brewery. For a time, people flocked to a glass office building in Clearwater, Florida to get a glimpse of a diaphanous shape on the side of the building that seemed to be the Virgin Mary.

The Church has always been cautious about the authenticity of supernatural phenomena and carefully investigates each claim. If, after examination, the Church does not find the claim to be harmful to the faithful, it may "recognize" the apparition—which in no way binds Catholics to "believe" in the appearance or any of the "messages." If the Church approves the apparition it may grant permission for public devotions at the site, allowing for Mary to be honored there in a special way.

Apparitions are private revelations and not doctrines of faith. No one is obliged to believe in apparitions; nor is one less Catholic by rejecting or being skeptical about them. There are some apparitions that have been approved by the Church, however, and have become popular pilgrimage sites, enriching the faith of millions around the world:

Our Lady of Guadalupe: In 1531 Mary appeared to Juan Diego in Tepeyac, Mexico, near Mexico City, and asked that a church be built on the spot. The local bishop, doubting Juan's tale, asked for a sign. Roses

Our Lady of...

and the image of Mary herself then appeared on Juan's cloak.

Today Our Lady of Guadalupe is honored especially among the Spanish and is considered the patroness of the Americas. Her image is revered, carried in processions, and prominently displayed on banners in churches.

Our Lady of the Miraculous Medal: In 1830 Mary appeared three times to a young novice, Catherine Laboure, in the chapel of the Daughters of Charity of Saint Vincent de Paul in Paris. Our Lady requested a medal be molded in honor of the Immaculate Conception. Today this medal is known as the Miraculous Medal because many healings have taken place through its use.

Our Lady of La Salette: Mary appeared to two teenagers in this remote French village in 1846. She was seated on a rock, weeping, and spoke to the youngsters of prayer, penance, and conversion. After five years of intense investigation, the local bishop recognized the apparition and the foundation was laid for a basilica to be built on the site.

Our Lady of Lourdes: The most famous vision of Mary occurred at Lourdes, France in 1858 to Bernadette Soubirous, a French peasant girl. Noted for its many healings and miraculous water from a nearby spring, Lourdes is probably the best known shrine of Mary's appearances. The event became popularized in the award-winning film, *The Song of Bernadette*.

Our Lady of Fatima: In 1917 Mary appeared to three children as they tended sheep in the countryside surrounding Fatima, Portugal. Mary identified herself as "Our Lady of the Rosary" and urged prayers, especially the rosary, for the conversion of sinners and the consecration of Russia to her Immaculate Heart.

Our Lady of Beauraing: During 1932-1933 in a school playground in Beauraing, Belgium, Mary began a series of appearances to five children. She told the children that she was the Immaculate Virgin and Mother of God, Queen of Heaven and called for penance and reparation for sinners.

Our Lady of Banneaux: In Banneaux, Belgium in 1933 Mary appeared eight times to Mariette Beco in a garden behind the family home. Mary promised, as "Virgin of the Poor," to intercede for the poor, the suffering, and the sick.

Still being evaluated by the Church, since 1981, are the alleged apparitions of Mary to six young people in Medjugorje, Yugoslavia. In recent years, pilgrims have come from all over the world to visit Medjugorje, and many books have been written about Mary's messages and the miracles that reportedly occur there. The Church considers these reports to be personal experiences, not authentic proofs or matters of faith.

Since there have been so many reports of visions and supernatural phenomena in recent years, the Congregation for the Doctrine of the Faith, in 1978, set up guidelines to assess alleged apparitions. The matter is first placed before the local bishop who decides whether to publicize the case. The facts are then assessed for truth and freedom of error. In this process, the alleged visionaries are studied for mental balance and integrity. For example, they cannot be reporting visions in such a way that promotes their own prestige or self-importance, such as financial advantages or other lucrative gains. The

Guidelines for Assessing Private Revelations

event cannot be considered a result of collective hysteria or mass hypnotic suggestion, and must enhance one's faith. It cannot condemn, ridicule, or criticize authentic Church doctrines and teachings.

Ultimately, all true devotion to Mary is rooted in Scripture and Tradition and leads to a closer relationship with Christ. If one's faith is increased by experiencing a supernatural occurrence, then there is merit in it. If pilgrims portray an attitude of prayer, penance, and frequenting of the sacraments, they are displaying commendable manifestations of faith, even though Church authorities may not publicly approve or support their experience.

Bear in mind that private revelations are just that—private—and no one is under obligation to participate in them or endorse them. A person is no less a devout Catholic if doubting or even rejecting approved apparitions or devotions to Mary.

Other Popular Devotions and Titles of Mary

True to the prophetic words, "All generations will call me blessed" (Luke 1:48), Mary has been honored in all climes and ages. Marian devotions and titles have become popular because of religious experiences or insights. Some well-known Marian titles include:

Our Lady of Knock: In August, 1879, fifteen people reported a vision of Mary, Joseph, and John the Evangelist on the wall of the village church at Knock, Ireland in the county of Mayo. Although the Church has not authenticated the vision, many healings have taken place there. Today Knock is a popular pilgrimage site with a magnificent basilica and has been visited by Pope John Paul II.

Our Lady of Czechstechowa: A popular icon reverenced by the Polish people is the Black Madonna, known as

Our Lady of Czestochowa. The icon, supposedly painted by Saint Luke and retrieved by Saint Helena, was brought to Poland and placed in a monastery of the Pauline Fathers in 1382. Marred by vandals, the icon was enshrined in Czestochowa in 1430 and has been given credit for the country's victory over Sweden in 1636. Today Our Lady of Czestochowa is honored as patroness of Poland.

Our Lady of Perpetual Help: One of the most familiar and famous icons of Mary is that of Our Lady of Perpetual Help. This work was taken from Crete and brought to Rome where it was enshrined in the Church of Saint Matthew in 1499. The icon was spared the French Revolution's pillaging of churches and was placed under the protection of the Redemptorist Fathers in Rome in 1866, with Pope Pius IX's instructions to "Make Our Mother of Perpetual Help known throughout the world." The image is of Mary and Jesus, both garbed in royal clothing and wearing crowns on their heads. Mary holds Jesus on her left arm and, in the background, are angels Michael and Gabriel, both holding the instruments of the crucifixion: cross, nails, lance, and vinegar vessel. Jesus, with both hands resting in Mary's right hand, looks back over his shoulder with fear, while Mary's piercing eyes solemnly look straight at the viewer. The icon and devotion to Our Lady of Perpetual Help is credited with many spiritual favors and miracles.

Our Lady of the Sacred Heart: Of specific interest to those who honor Jesus' compassionate love as the Sacred Heart is a parallel devotion to Mary, Our Lady of the Sacred Heart. From Mary, Christ received his physical being, and it is through her that we come to Jesus. When we reflect on Christ's love, we open ourselves to let Mary show us the way to imitate the heart of Christ. The image of Our Lady of the Sacred Heart depicts Mary holding the child Jesus on her left arm. Jesus holds his heart in one hand and points to Mary with his other, as if to say, "If you want to be close to me, remember my mother." (A more contemporary image of Our Lady of the Sacred Heart depicts Mary contemplating the pierced heart of Christ on the cross.)

Mary as Our Lady of the Sacred Heart—the inspiration of Father Jules Chevalier—is honored especially by the religious communities founded on Chevalier's charism: Missionaries of the Sacred Heart (Fathers and Brothers), Missionary Sisters of the Most Sacred Heart, and Daughters of Our Lady of the Sacred Heart.

The basilica in honor of Our Lady of the Sacred Heart at Issoudun, France is, after Lourdes, the second largest Marian pilgrimage site in France.

Marian Shrines in the United States

Throughout the United States, thousands of churches, institutions, schools, colleges, hospitals, and entire towns bear the name of Mary. In the 188 Catholic dioceses, 56 cathedrals are named in honor of Mary. The oldest cathedral in the United States, located in Baltimore, was dedicated to Mary's Assumption long before the dogma was proclaimed. Pope John Paul II honored this shrine on a recent visit to the United States.

Likewise, many parish churches are named in honor of Mary. My home diocese serves as a measuring stick of the prevalence of Marian parish churches. Of the 153 parishes in the Allentown, Pennsylvania diocese, 40 parishes are dedicated to Mary. So if this ratio holds true, of the more than nineteen thousand parishes in the United States, several thousand are probably dedicated to Mary.

National Shrine of the Immaculate Conception: Among the monuments outstanding in our nation's capital is the

Basilica of the National Shrine of the Immaculate Conception. It ranks as the eighth largest church in the world and the largest in the Western Hemisphere. Its azure dome and impressive campanile and bell tower, dominating the otherwise flat skyline of Washington D.C., symbolize the significant role Mary plays in our nation's history. Its numerous chapels pay tribute to the many titles and ethnic heritages by which Mary is revered by American Catholics.

Shrine of the Immaculate Heart of Mary: The Blue Army, with headquarters and a magnificent shrine in Washington, New Jersey, is the World Center for the Apostolate of Fatima, and propagates the message and mission of Fatima.

Mary, Queen of the Universe Shrine: This exquisite church serves as a spiritual oasis for the Disney World tourists in Orlando, Florida.

Our Lady of the Rockies Shrine: High in the mountains on the Continental Divide, 8,510 feet above sea level, overlooking Butte, Montana, is a ninety-foot statue of Mary, Mother of Jesus. The massive image was built in response to a promise made by a grateful husband whose wife returned to health. The project took six years to complete and today stands as a nondenominational tribute to Mary and all women, especially mothers.

Grotto of the Redemption: Located in West Bend, Iowa, this shrine, made out of stone, depicts many biblical scenes and is an impressive creative monument to Christian faith.

Other national shrines to Our Lady include:

Our Lady of La Leche, St. Augustine, Florida
Our Lady of the Snows, Belleville, Illinois
National Shrine of Our Lady of Prompt Succor, New Orleans, Louisiana
National Shrine Grotto of Our Lady of Lourdes, Emmitsburg, Maryland
National Shrine of Our Lady of La Salette, Ipswich, Massachusetts
National Shrine of the Miraculous Medal, Perryville, Missouri
National Shrine of Our Lady Help of Christians, West Haverstraw, New York
Our Lady of Fatima National Shrine Basilica, Youngstown, New York ·
Our Lady of Victory National Shrine, Lackawanna, New York
Basilica and National Shrine of Our Lady of Consolation, Carey, Ohio
National Shrine, Our Lady of Lebanon, North Jackson, Ohio
National Shrine of Our Lady of Czestochowa, Doylestown, Pennsylvania
National Shrine Center of Our Lady of Guadalupe, in Immaculate Conception Church, Allentown, Pennsylvania
National Shrine of Mary, Help of Christians, Holy Hill-Hubertus, Wisconsin

Worth special mention is the Marian library at the University of Dayton, under the direction of the Marianists. This facility has been under development for the past fifty years and boasts one of the world's largest collections of Marian treasures including a collection of Marian literature in over fifty languages. As a research center, the library offers information, courses, and newsletters, making it a major center of Mariological studies.

- The Immaculate Conception is not synonymous with the Virgin Birth. Mary conceived without the stain of original sin is the Immaculate Conception, whereas the Virgin Birth affirms that Mary, although giving birth to Jesus, remained a virgin.

- In Loreto, Italy, on the Adriatic Coast, stands a stone structure—the Holy House of Loreto—believed to be Mary's house in Nazareth. Tradition has it that this structure was transported by angels to three other sites before alighting in Loreto. The tale is pure legend, but because the site has inspired much devotion, it has been a minor basilica since 1728.

- Contrary to popular opinion, the state of Maryland is not named for the Blessed Mother. Rather, the state is named after Queen Henrietta Marie, wife of King Charles I.

- "Mary" and derivatives thereof are the most popular names given to girls.

- Besides Mary, the mother of Jesus, there are six other Marys in the New Testament: (1) Mary Magdalen, the penitent, (2) Mary, sister of Lazarus, (3) Mary, mother of James, (4) Mary, wife of Clophas, (5) Mary, mother of John, (6) Mary greeted by Paul in Romans 16:6.

- Mary is highly revered in Islam. The revelations to Muhammad between 610 and 632, recorded in the Koran, are considered by Muslims to be the very voice of God. The nineteenth surah is titled "Miryam" and is the only surah devoted to a specific woman. It speaks of Mary as the "bearer of the Word of God," the Virgin Mother of Jesus whom Muslims honor as a prophet preceding Muhammad.

- The pass thrown into the end zone in hopes of scoring a touchdown in the game of football is called a Hail Mary pass because of a desperate need to score points.

Mary: Woman of All Ages and Nations

In this day and age, when the world seems to be shrinking and we are exposed to people of all cultures, Mary is no less multicultural and a "woman for all nations." If we peruse the numerous images of Mary and how various countries portray her in their art, we can readily sense that all peoples claim Mary as one of their own. Our American culture often pictures Mary as a blue-eyed beauty with long flowing blond tresses. Orientals don Mary in voluminous kimonos and give her the typical oriental look: slanted eyes and dark hair. In India's art, Mary wears a colorful sari.

Catholics look to Mary as a staunch woman of faith, the ideal Christian who guides and directs us. We honor her because she is so authentically human, so ordinary in her extraordinary role, so within the reach of anyone who calls on her.

Mary symbolizes and portrays all that is wholesome and desirous. Mary is the epitome of feminine graciousness, the embodiment of all virtues, the model of one who lived the human condition most faithfully and fully, replete with hardships, sufferings, and confusions. In a world rife with antipathy and violence, in a world that idolizes the raunchy, Mary stands out as a beacon of hope. Her virtues and goodness radiate into all the facets of human life and affect every human endeavor.

If in our daily affairs we can assume the stance and

attitude of Mary, the world will become the haven of peace and love for which we all yearn. Mary's life of quiet, humble dedication is the ideal toward which we all strive in our earthly sojourn.

Mary's mind and attitude can be ours if we reflect on and act the way Mary did. After all, Mary is larger than our rote prayers and devotionals. Even though an explanation of her life is sparse, we have enough scriptural, traditional, and historical background on which to fashion a Marian model for our own lives of faith.

Every corner of this world needs to be touched by the same motherly care Mary lavished on Jesus. As we continue the work of her Son, Mary watches and guards the People of God. That is why we call Mary truly the "Mother of the Church."

Mary, who so easily assumes the faces of many nations and cultures, serves as a bridge-builder to the next millennium, spanning ages, generations, cultures, and individual spiritualities. She fits in wherever the human heart allows. Mary as the "Woman for All Nations and All Seasons" is always relevant, always in style, always ready to be a powerful advocate in human needs and concerns. Look to Mary as the bastion of integrity, the ideal of openness and flexibility, the authentic Christian who paves the way for all of us, one "whom we all call Blessed."

About the Author

 Sister Charlene Altemose, MSC, is a Missionary Sister of the Most Sacred Heart (Reading, Pennsylvania) with degrees in education, theology, and journalism. Her ministries have included teaching college theology, writing newspaper columns and articles, directing parish adult education, and being active in interfaith activities and the Council of Churches.

Sister Charlene was awarded a Fullbright scholarship to India and a Christian Leadership grant to Israel. As a result of her scholarship excellence, she was invited to be a presenter at the 1993 Council for a Parliament of World Religions.

Author of Liguori's popular *What You Should Know About...* series (*What You Should Know About the Mass; What You Should Know About the Catechism of the Catholic Church; What You Should Know About the Sacraments; What You Should Know About Angels; What You Should Know About the Saints*), Sister Charlene is a popular speaker at workshops, retreats, and in-service or adult education programs.

More "What You Should Know About..." titles
by Charlene Altemose, MSC

WHAT YOU SHOULD KNOW ABOUT ANGELS

A fascinating look at how angels make their presence known to us, and how Catholics can include angels in daily worship and personal spirituality. **$4.95**

WHAT YOU SHOULD KNOW ABOUT
THE CATECHISM OF THE CATHOLIC CHURCH

An absolutely indispensable starting point for basic understanding, intelligent reading, and practical use of the *Catechism of the Catholic Church.* **$1.95**
Also available in Spanish...
Lo Que Usted Debe Saber Sobre el Catecismo de la Iglesia Católica **$1.95**

WHAT YOU SHOULD KNOW ABOUT THE MASS

This popular title covers the role played by those present and the symbolic gestures used in the Mass, outlines the liturgical seasons, and details each section of the Mass. **$3.95**
Also available in Spanish...
Lo Que Usted Debe Saber Sobre Misa **$3.95**

WHAT YOU SHOULD KNOW ABOUT
THE SACRAMENTS

Each sacrament is discussed in light of specific issues of present-day sacramental practice and ways in which the celebrations of the sacraments can be alive and vibrant. **$3.95**
Also available in Spanish...
Lo Que Usted Debe Saber Sobre los Sacramentos **$3.95**

WHAT YOU SHOULD KNOW ABOUT THE SAINTS

A fascinating look at the history, tradition, and Church teaching about the Saints. Sprinkled with an abundance of little-known facts, this book presents a reliable study of the Saints. **$4.95**

Order from your local bookstore or write to:
Liguori Publications
Box 060, Liguori, MO 63057-9999
Please add 15% to your total for shipping and handling
($3.50 minimum, $15 maximum).
For faster service, call toll-free 1-800-325-9521, Dept. 060.
Please have your credit card handy.